# THE OLD MARKET SQUARE AND THE MARTYRDOM OF JOAN OF ARC

ISBN 2-85480-653-0

OLIVIER CHALINE

# THE OLD MARKET SQUARE AND THE MARTYRDOM OF JOAN OF ARC

ÉDITIONS
Charles CORLET
Z.I., route de Vire
14110 Condé-sur-Noireau

*The rehabilitation cross*

# PREFACE

1979-1999 : it has already been twenty years that the Sainte-Jeanne-d'Arc church has fit into the layout of the Old-Market square.

Twenty years already that the church is back in the square, with its pedestrian precinct, its shops and its market.

Twenty years already that the Christian community of the neighbourhood is back in its parish church, after Saint-Sauveur, destroyed two centuries ago, and then Saint-Vincent, wiped out in 1944.

Twenty years already that, every year, hundreds of thousands of visitors and pilgrims go through the door of this haven of peace to gaze at the tapestry of stained-glass windows indicated in most tourist guides worldwide.

Twenty years already that Joan of Arc, a national heroine and a saint, has been honoured as she should be on the very site of her death.

This beautiful church stands next to the memorial and to the rehabilitation cross. Awaited for decades by many inhabitants of Rouen, we owe it to the stubborn will of a mayor, Mr Jean Lecanuet, to the genius of an architect, Mr Louis Arretche, and to the expertise of contractors, master glaziers, artisans, sculptors, Compagnons du Devoir and of workers in the building trade.

I have asked Mr Olivier Chaline, a historian, *agrégé* of the University, professor at the Ecole normale supérieure de la rue d'Ulm, to write the following pages.

Our old friendship, his attachment to the city of Rouen and his expertise have guided my choice.

The following pages are to help the reader or the visitor, whether from Rouen or just visiting, understand and appreciate better this truly attaching neighbourhood of our town, the treasures of our truly modern church made with old materials but also the mystery of saint-Joan-of-Arc.

We would like to thank Mr Olivier Chaline for this testimony of fervour.

We would like his work to contribute towards making this church a Mecca of the memory of Saint Joan of Arc and of the prayer and opening to all men.

Philippe POIRSON, priest,
Parish priest of Sainte-Jeanne-d'Arc.

*Statue of Joan of Arc by Real del Sarte*

# THE OLD MARKET SQUARE AND THE MARTYRDOM OF JOAN OF ARC

## *The martyrdom*

Joan of Arc was captured in Compiègne on the 23rd May 1430 during an unfortunate outing, she was then handed over to the British by the Duke of Burgundy thanks to the intervention of the bishop of Beauvais, Pierre Cauchon. Joan of Arc arrived in Rouen around Christmas. Most of the inhabitants of the town which had become British since 1419 were unaware of her presence and had never even heard of her. The lasting settling of the British system of government had given rise to more resistance in the country than in the Norman capital. The prisoner was detained in a tower that no longer exists restored at the end of the 19th Century at the top of the rue Jeanne-d'Arc, near the station. Her trial was both religious and political, with repeated legal irregularities, the charge – heresy - being clearly religious, just as the formation of the court made up of Church people, but it was not questionable that the stake was political. Instead of being kept in a church prison, Joan of Arc was placed under the supervision of English gaolers. She was to be tried as a witch for she embodied resistance to the English dynasty and proclaimed the divine support to Charles VII. The King of France seemed to have let down the woman who had him sacred in Rheims. The trial

started on the 9th January and ended, after all sorts of incidences, by the torture of the stake on the 30th May 1431.

*The stocks*

Three scaffolds had been put up on the Market square, the first one against the market so that canon Nicolas Midi, from the university of Paris competent in matters of heresy and pro-English, pronounce a speech and two other ones near the cemetery of Saint-Sauveur for the judges and royal officers who came and sat around 9 in the morning. Finally a stake awaited Joan who was read the sentence : "We have, by fair sentence, declared that you, Joan, commonly called the Maid of Orleans, have committed different errors and various crimes of schism, idolatry, invocation of demons and many others. We consider you are heretic and hereby we decide that, such as a rotten limb, you must be expelled from the unity of the Church and abandoned to secular power." However, she was granted communion although she had been excommunicated. She went to her death, with "pious and devout lamentations and invocations of the blessed Trinity and of the blessed glorious Virgin Mary and all the blessed saints of heaven (...) asking for pardon very humbly to all kinds of people (...) both on her side and on the other one, asking them to pray for her, forgiving the evil they had done to her."

At the foot of the stake, "she asked for a cross and an Englishman who was present made a little one in wood he gave it to her and devoutly she received it and kissed it, and put the cross on her bosom, between her skin and her clothes."

One of the closest witnesses was the Dominican brother Isambart, from the neighbouring convent of Saint-Jacques, who attended her last moments.

"Joan said such devout, pious and Catholic words that all those who watched her and who were in large numbers, cried so hard and therefore the cardinal of England and several other Englishmen were forced to cry and to have compassion.

The pious woman asked me, beseeched and implored me, as I was near her and she was about to die - to go to the closest church and to bring her the cross so that it be held high before her eyes until her death, so that the cross on which God was hung was in her life continuously before her eyes. And furthermore, being inside the flame, she never stopped, even at the end, proclaiming and confessing aloud the saint name of Jesus, by imploring and invoking continuously the help of the saints of heaven ; and also, what is more, when she breathed her last and tilted her head, she uttered the name of Jesus to show she was fervent in the faith of God.

Forthwith after the execution, the executioner came to see me and my companion brother Martin Ladvenu, struck and moved by such marvellous penitence and terrible contrition, as any desperate, fearing to never be able to ask for pardon and indulgence to God for what he had done to this saint woman. And the executioner said and asserted that notwithstanding the oil, the sulfur and the coal he had applied on the entrails and the heart of Joan, he had not been able at all to burn nor put in cinders her entrails nor her heart, and he was quite astonished as if it were an obvious miracle."

They hurried and threw the remains in the Seine river and the Rouen inhabitants, after the moment of emotion caused by this unusual death of a quite pious witch, forgot for several centuries - unlike the inhabitants of Orléans - Joan of Arc's existence. The procedures of the trial of rehabilitation open at the request of the family in 1455 changed nothing of this indifference, despite the cassation and the cancellation of the sentence of 1431, on the 7th July 1456 in the great room of the palace of the archbishop. There were other executions and many other markets held on the square, without there being erected the expiatory cross planned in 1456.

## *The tranformations of the square*

There were not many squares in the medieval town encircled with walls, and this gave a special appeal to this area which remained open, despite multiple encroachments of the layout since the 13th century. From the end of the Middle Ages to the mid 19th century, it kept an irregular trapezoid shape between rue Cauchoise leading to the pays de Caux and rue du Gros-Horloge leading to the cathedral and to the Pont sur la Seine (bridge over the Seine river). With the place de la Haute-Vieille Tour between the cathedral and the Seine river, it was one of the most busy points of the town where countryfolk and city dwellers met. Southwards, the parrishes of tradesmen went to the Seine river, saint-Vincent, saint-Eloi notably. The rue du Vieux-Palais still gives an idea of this part of the town which disappeared between 1940 and 1944. Northwards was the quietest neighbourhood of the magistrates with streets lined with town houses close to the Saint-Patrice church. But the square was devoted to the trade of foodstuffs – poultry, herbs, vegetables, fish, pigs... and this intense activity extended to the many inns in the neighbourhood. In addition to the markets, the crowds gathered together to see the executions of legal sentences, a highly prized show.

The main monuments of the square were – with the covered market – the two churches of Saint-Sauveur and Saint-Michel, flanked by small cemeteries. The first one had Pierre Corneille, the writer, among its treasurers, from 1649 to 1651. Today only its foundations remain which were cleared during the construction work of the present church of Sainte Jeanne-d'Arc. The other church, Saint-Michel, was just at the entrance of the rue du Gros-Horloge.

In 1749, the architect Mathieu Le Carpentier planned to remodel the square by doubling its surface area, in order to erect on the west side a monumental classic town hall whose central pavilion would have been topped by a dome.The model can still be seen in the Fine Arts museum. From the Old Market square, an entire part of the town was remodelled, since a large rectilineous street was planned leading to the cathedral, after the destruction of the Gros Horloge (Big

Clock) and of the wooden-side houses. The surroundings of the new square adorned in its centre with a statue of Louis 15$^{th}$, would also be rebuilt. The work was started in 1757 but was stopped two years later, for lack of money, leaving huge incompleted foundations, still visible rue de la Pie.

The square's appearance stopped changing until the Revolution and at that period the trade eliminate all religious presence. Saint-Sauveur, closed in 1791, served for just a short time as a saltpetre plant then was razed to the ground in 1795, whereas Saint-Michel was turned into a shop then turned again in 1833 into a residential property. As the century went along, more or less covered and sturdy markets followed one another. Covered markets and metal pavilions were finally inaugurated in 1867 and the square's surface area was doubled by the destruction of all its north and north-east side. No rules were imposed for the rebuilding of the square. Foodstuffs shops and the French Theatre occupied it and there were no more changes until the 1920's.

## *The late commemoration of Joan of Arc*

In the 1920's Joan of Arc was beatified and then canonized and this resulted in changes in the layout of the square. It took a lot of time to remember the Maid of Orleans, and it took even more time for this concern to be connected with the Old-Market square. Since the 15$^{th}$ century, the site of her death had even been forgotten, and therefore in the 18$^{th}$ century, when Joan of Arc was rediscovered, her statue was set up on the neighbouring square called the Marché-aux-Veaux, today called la Pucelle. The sculptor Slodtz represented her in 1754 under the features of Bellone, but the 1944 bombings were fatal to it. The heroine of the struggle against England was rediscovered little by little during the 18$^{th}$ century, marked after 1744 by an intermittent fight against England. In the 1840's, the publication of the documents of the trial and the romantic period increased the interest in her, without any concern for the Old-Market square, since the statue of Joan of Arc was set up at the town hall. The priority at that time was to save the dungeon of the castle of Philippe August. In September 1870, the town council took advantage of the fall of the Second Empire to turn rue de l'Impératrice into rue Jeanne-d'Arc. It was only at the end of the century that there was an official interest in the heroine. In 1891, her beatification was introduced before the court of Rome, which was accepted in 1909, and from 1892, near the pilgrimage church of Bonsecours, a monument to Joan of Arc was erected which towers above the town. However there was no national holiday until 1920. From 1896-1897, the *Union Jeanne d'Arc* organized a special celebration in Rouen and since 1900 a spray is placed every year place du Vieux-Marché.

During World War One, soldiers worshipped Joan of Arc. She was canonized in 1920 after the victory. The national holiday was promulgated on the $10^{th}$ July. The sculptor Real del Sarte gave in 1926 a statue of Joan. Various projects were devised, from the limited conversion to the large-scope replanning of the square and some even spoke about erecting a basilica.

A temporary small chapel was set up rue de Crosne. Two different projects of memorials were examined before 1931, envisaging a large church with a spire. Finally, according to the architect Lair's plan, the southern market was reduced by two western bays replaced by a fake façade in Norman and medieval style, with stone arches and on the ground level the statue and a level with wooden sides. On the $30^{th}$ May 1931, was celebrated with splendour the $500^{th}$ anniversary of her martyrdom.

Without being as hit by the bombs than other neighbourhoods of the town, the square was damaged during the war. More to the south, the Saint-Vincent church was almost totally destroyed. Parishioners had to take refuge in the small chapel of Sainte-Jeanne-d'Arc.

*Bust of Joan of Arc by Real del Sarte*

*Saint-Vincent – Panelling of the choir*

# THE CHURCH OF SAINT-JOAN-OF-ARC

## *The legacy of Saint-Vincent*

Only ruins were left of the Saint-Vincent church demolished in part by the opening of a new street and of stained-glass windows that had been removed and put in a safe place at the beginning of the war. But at first they had not planned to replace them. These stained-glass windows testified to the artistic quality of the former building. Testified to since the 12th century, the Saint-Vincent parish, close to the Seine river, was inhabited, towards 1500 by tradesmen. Rouen was then one of the main French ports, in full expansion when sea routes towards the New World were open. Norman tradesmen and sailors traded with Brazil, with Antwerp and northern countries as well as with Spain. The receipts drawn from the sale of salt helped to erect in the 16th century a beautiful building in flamboyant gothic style which, if it still existed – would be the matching piece to Saint-Maclou. The choir started to be rebuilt in 1515 and the church was consecrated in 1531. Probably the extent of the project exceeded the income of the parish and therefore the church never got a nave as high as the choir and had to do without a spire on its tower. However, thanks to the generosity of its parishioners it was fitted with high quality stained-glass windows. Later, in the 18th century, it was ornated with a rich rococo-style inside decoration, that, unfortunately, was completely destroyed by the bombing on 31st May 1944.

## *Eventually a church*

As none of the plans prior to 1939 succeeded, other projects followed one another without any more success. The decision to transfer the central covered market to a market-station a long way from the town centre contributed towards simplifying the problem. Everyone finally agreed on building a long church at the southern end of the square and on erecting a small covered market adjoining it to the north, a large cross indicating the site of the stake. At the end of 1977 the façades of the wooden-sided houses that had been demolished in the eastern neighbourhoods of the town were erected again on the south west side of the square.

*One of the many fountains of Rouen*

The church was designed by the architect Louis Arretche who drew his inspiration for the design of the vault from the hull of a ship turned upside down. Consacrated on the 29th April 1979 by Mgr Pailler, archbishop of Rouen, the church is 40 metres long and 28 metres high. It has the shape of a flame, whereas the neighbouring market recall the waves.

*Church lit at night*

*The baptistry*

South, a large slate roof decorated with copper flakes towers above a wall with two fish-shaped windows, whereas on the north east side there are windows which give onto a garden and are lit at night. The porch is open on the west side, on the side of the gallery in which there is an inscription of André Malraux on Joan of Arc : "Joan, without a sepulchre and without a portrait, you who knew that the tomb of the heroines is the heart of the living." From the entrance, you can simultaneously see the sanctuary and the stained-glass windows. The vault is made of fir strips and a framework of metal pipes which give it its thrust. The only column of the building is close to the high altar in repoussé gold pewter, made by Kaeppelin. The paving is in bricks which go from black to red

*Detail of the roof structure*

*A Sunday mass*

as you get closer to the altar. The congregation sit on teak benches laid in a semicircle. A side chapel, decorated by Hess, houses the old panelling from the ruins of Saint-Vincent. But the old church is especially present by its beautiful windows thanks to the persistence of an old Rouen inhabitant, Mrs Néel, attached to the heritage of her town.

*Chapel of the Saint-Sacrament*

## *The stained-glass windows*

They form a whole because they all were in the choir of Saint-Vincent and date back from the 1520-1530's. We only know the precise year of one of them, *The life of Saint-John the-Baptist* of 1526.

### *Achievement*

Stained-glass windows are made in several stages. The first one is the difficult making of the glass in glass factories close to forests. The molten glass which is cooked is made of two thirds of plant cinders (potassium, wood, soda, fern and heather) and one third of washed river sand (for silica). The whole is brought to high temperature to the fusion. Save in the case of the red shade, the molten glass is coloured by adding metal oxides. Then to give it a shape and transparency, it is blown either by muff or by panel. The future stained-glass window can then be made, and first a model of it gives an idea of it to the persons who ordered it. A cardboard is made which is a sketch of the size of the window, with layout and colours, which will be used as a guide. Parts are numbered then templates in cardboard are cut out which will be used to cut out the glass with a diamond. The panel is then coloured according to the transparency of the glasses which depends on their location in the opening.If the translucence must be modified, painting will be applied. Since the start of the $14^{th}$ century, gold yellow is cold-applied on the outside surface. Engraving allows to modify the colouring of the glasses by attacking them with acid to obtain shaded tones. This is carried out on plated glasses after removing the coloured layer. It must be cooked around 600° for gold yellow and grisaille. Then there is the lead glazing then putty is placed under the leads for tightness. The windows must then be placed in the opening divided into panels separated by networks of stone, called fillers. These are completed by a frame in iron bars in which the panels are slid. At regular intervals, small round iron bars appear held by fasteners welded to the leads.

Throughout northern France and particularly Normandy, the first half of the 16th century was a great period for stained-glass windows. Technical improvements modified the glass-makers' work, such as the diamond cutting and no longer the branding iron, and the paint. The grisaille, the gold yellow or the red chalk allowed to vary the shades. It was a period of varied and neat compositions, sometimes decorated with inlays which enriched the decor. It was also the influence of Flemish painting which, since the middle of the previous century, caused the renewal of the decors. The same composition was on the entire bay window and the architectural decor of the scene represented was put in perspective. Most often there were landscapes with a lot of shades plus many familiar touches and details. Inspiration was drawn from prints that were widely distributed thanks to the printing industry, and expressed both the Italian architectural repertoire (Roman temples, arcs of triumph) and the compositions of the German painter and engraver Albrecht Dürer which, for part, inspired the *vitrail des chars* of Saint-Vincent. The windows are sub-divided into several registers with compartments between which appears the same story, and even the same scene. Often, inscriptions on string courses allow to identify the scene represented more easily.

In the church there are two sets of glasses. The first one was made by the workshop of the Le Prince de Beauvais family. Engrand (who died in 1531) and Jean Le Prince were active between 1491 and 1555. The first one signed *Le vitrail des chars* (with Jean), *La vie de Saint Jean-Baptiste* and *Les œuvres de Miséricorde*. The Le Princes left works with highly skillful techniques and with a large variety of shades and colours. "With his animated compositions, marked by the dynamism of characters which is expressed by their dancing look or by their expressive attitude", Engrand "brings, notes F. Perrot, an unequalled sophistication in the technique of painting. The contours are worked on a quite thick grisaille washing (attacked with a hard brush at right angles to the glass), then lightened by needle or by cross bar (...). There are very few full lines, only to draw precise contours. On a same piece, the net oppositions between several values of grisaille of different colours – black or reheated with red chalk which give it a red shade – are enough to mark the outline of the objects or to represent the incessant movement of the hangs and the crumpling of the fabrics. But Engrand is a true master when he uses silver yellow and draws at once all kinds of motifs on the character's clothes, having the copperware of the decor or of the costumes shine brightly (…), or also completes the contours with grisaille, on the edge of a white collar or on a coloured piece (…). Several values of silver yellow, from lemon to orange are used on the same piece, making a contour as on the wonderful bird which flies over the audience of the sermon of saint John the Baptist."

Another workshop, in Rouen this time, produced ten windows which distinguished themselves by the extent of the architectural decor and the concern for the preciseness of the faces. Their authors were probably marked by the stained-glass windows made by one of the most famous master glaziers of the time – Arnoult de Nimègue.

## *Description of the stained-glass windows (from left to right)*

1 – *Saint Peter's life*. It is the latest of the windows of the Rouen series. It is made up of two registers with four scenes in the lancets. At the bottom left, Christ calls to him the two fishermen, Peter and Andrew, represented with their small craft and their nets. Then there is the episode of the miraculous draught of fishes, Peter and another apostle pulling the nets while Christ is standing in the craft. Far away, ships appear. Peter is then confronted with Simon, the magician. The apostle lists on his fingers the arguments in his favour. His opponent tears his books and, abandoned by the demons, falls from the Capitol. In the background appear the churches of Saint-Ouen and Saint-Maclou of Rouen. At the top left appears the sermon of Peter who, then, cures the sick and the disabled. Then comes the delivery of the keys by Christ and finally the scene of "*Domine, quo vadis*", when Peter, leaving Rome and the persecution, meets Christ who encourages him to go back to town. The manner the faces are painted is similar to those

made by the master glazier Arnoult de Nimègue because thin hatchings substitute to the features and give the facial appearances a special delicacy. Other episodes of Saint Peter's life are represented in the tympan of the window (walk on the waves, resurrection of the little girl Tabitha, meeting with Christ, delivery by the angel and crucifixion in the middle of the angels), but this part only dates back from 1869.

*Saint Peter's life*

*Detail of the stained-glass window of the life of Saint Peter*

*Detail of the stained-glass window*
*of Saint Anne*

2 – *Saint Anne and Saint Joachim*, the parents of the Virgin Mary. To the left, an angel, wings spread and carrying a sealed contract, announces to Joachim the shepherd, in the middle of his flock, the birth of Mary. Under the trees, a shepherd is playing bagpipes. At the Golden Door in Jerusalem, represented as an arc of triumph of the Renaissance with a harrow but pilasters and profile medallions, Joachim meets Anne. The birth of the Virgin shows a scene of a child birth with the women around the bed and the bath of the child, a representation which can be compared with the one of the birth of saint Roman at the cathedral. The Virgin then enters the Temple. The great priest is at the top of the stairs, an altar appears under the vault, with a canopy, an altarpiece in plate and sculptures. Many onlookers follow the parents. Finally, the tympan is occupied by the story of the hanged man unhanged thanks to saint Jacques, told in the *Golden legend* by Jacques de Voragine and dear to the pilgrims of Compostela.

3 – *The triumph of the Virgin* or *the vitrail des chars*. Here the theme is the Immaculate Conception which was not yet a dogma but was vividly discussed between theologians, Francicans being very attached to it and Dominicans opposed. The tympan shows the Trinity (the Father, the Son, and the Holy Spirit) with the Virgin, represented by a little girl reading in the book the 23rd verse of chapter 8 of the book of Proverbs : "I have been established since eternity and from the start, before earth was created." The other openwork of the tympan are the Creator Word with the Virgin, the chaos of the origins, heaven and earth with the twelve signs of the Zodiac and the woman taken from Adam's rib, according to the book of the Genesis. The stained-glass window is then made up of three superimposed registers. First of all, the triumph of Adam and Eve, naked on a chariot, in the middle of the luxuriant vegetation of heaven, with birds and various animals, including a unicorn. The sun and the moon also appear. Adam is holding the standard of justice, while the chariot bears the inscription : "*Omnia subjecisti sub pedibus ejus* (You submitted everything to it)", a quotation from Psalm 8. The chariot is drawn by strength accompanied by faith which holds a church. Behind the chariot come the charity with the sun, the temperance

*The triumph of the Virgin or the vitrail des chars*

with a death's-head, hope and wisdom. The third lancet bears at the top the words which apply once again to the Virgin, "*Nonquam erant abyssae etiam concepta eram*" (Even before the abymes, I had been conceived)", Proverb 8, 24.

To happiness in heaven follows the fall represented in the median row of the window. Adam and Eve are chained up by work and pain, a quotation from Psalm 89 used as a comment : "The large number of years is only sorrow and suffering." The triumph is hence the triumph of the tempting snake whose chariot is decorated with the standard of disobedience and accompanied by credulity which seized the broken standard of justice. The angels flee, leaving the place to the seven capital sins.

But the lower register represents the redemption of humanity thanks to the Virgin, new Eve, mother of the saviour of mankind. A quotation from the Song of Songs clearly indicates the Immaculate Conception (the Virgin conceived without sin) : "You are beautiful, my friend and stainless." The chariot of the Virgin crushes the demon, according to the verse of the Genesis (III, 15) about Eve and the snake : "The snake will crush your head", now applied to the Virgin. The angels, who are back, pull the chariot preceded by the prophet Isaiah and king David. At the head of the procession, Moses holds a stick with the bronze snake which here is a figure heralding crucified Christ, allusion to an episode of the exodus : in the camp of Israel invaded by snakes, survived those who looked at the bronze snake made by Moses. Truth is on a unicorn, symbol of virginity, and holds a standard representing the dove of the Holy Saint. At the bottom left of the scene, appear Rouen bourgeois praying : "God, help me, protect your servant who has hope in you." It is possible to compare the triumph of the Virgin with the one which decorates the north bottom side of the Saint-Patrice church in Rouen.

4 – *Saint Anne's tree*, also called verrière des Trois Marie, draws its theme from the *Golden legend* and from the vision of saint Colette de Corbie, the reformer of the Poor Clare in the $15^{th}$ century. It is about the three marriages of saint Anne with whom she had three daughters, the Virgin Mary, Mary Cleophas and Mary Salome. The children of the last two ones were almost all apostles around Christ, son of Mary the elder. This genealogy at that time in favour was - a few decades after the window was made - rejected by the humanists, then by protestant reformers and the partisans of a refined catholicism after the Council of Trent. It is represented here in the same manner as Jesse's, the founder being at the bottom. The trunk goes from saint Anne who is teaching the Virgin Mary how to read. A lancet is devoted to each branch – Mary Jacobe on the left, Mary Salome on the right. The median level is devoted to the Virgin Mary and to Jesus, with, on the left, saint James with his stick, saint John with a chalice of poison tranformed into a demon. Labels were inverted and therefore they are presented as the sons of Mary Cleophas but are in fact Mary Salome's

*Saint Anne's tree*

sons. On the right, the four sons of Mary Cleophas stand, notably saint James the Minor with his fuller's stick and saint Jude with a procession cross. A chorus of angels appears in the tympan, and at the lower level, donors surround the scene of the meeting of Anne and Joachim at the Golden door.

5 – *The life of saint John the Baptist,* of 1526, is the only dated stained-glass window. It can be read from top to bottom and from left to right with, in the tympan, an angel who appears to Zachary the priest standing before the altar of the Temple of Jerusalem. The Visitation of the Virgin Mary to her cousin Elizabeth is represented on the right. In the lower register, one can recognize John the Baptist dressed as a prophet, leaving his parents then his sermon to the crows to whom he designates Christ : "Here is the Lamb of God." There are four

*Life of saint John the Baptist*

scenes in the lancets : the sermon of John the Baptist in the middle of the forest with men and animals (top left), the baptism of Christ (right) with two angels holding the tunic of Christ and the Word of the Father "Here is my beloved Son who has all my favour", then, at the bottom, in continuation, the martyrdom with the beheading and Salome bringing the head to her mother. When it was restored in the 19th century, the chronological and causal order was inverted by the transformation of the last scene into the dance of Salome. The strong unity of composition of this very meticulous window is due to two factors – the vegetation of the upper landscape and the architecture of the lower register.

6 – The theme of the *œuvres de Miséricorde* are the words of Christ (Matthew, XXV, 35-36). The narrow window is made of a single lancet in four superimposed scenes of three panels each. At the bottom there is the feast of the bad rich man flanked by self-importance on the right, a nun and a poor man on the left. Two inscriptions indicate : "*Frenata est in pauperta-vs*

*mea* (my poverty has been curbed *)" and "Po(ri)ge esurie(n) ti pane(m) tuum (*give your bread to one who has not). Above, pity is represented under the features of a young woman who speaks to Christ in favour of two rich men : "*Dic ut lapides isti panes fiant* (turn these stones into bread)." But to these ungrateful persons, Christ answers : "They will suffer from hunger as dogs." On the left, death sticks its arrow in the chest of one of the lying men, showing it is both for the rich and the poor, as the inscription says. In the background of the third scene, charity assists the poor : "I will satisfy the poor with bread." On the left, wealth pushes necessity away with its children : "The children have asked for bread, woe betide those who will push them away", whereas on the right, a purse in the head, charity pours water on the flames ready to consume a lying man : "Just as water puts out the fire, charity puts out sin." The forefront is occupied by another inscription : "They have huge wealths and are starving "

The tympan offers a complex composition with many characters with other inscriptions. But Christ is in the centre, distributing the bread, commented as follows : "Stand up after sitting to eat the bread of pain" and "come to me, flock who work and are overwhelmed, and I will satisfy you". From the left, suddenly appear penitents ("You will feed us with bread"), ignorants ("You will feed us with the bread of life and spirit") and destitutes ("Give us our daily bread"), while come from the right, health ("I reddened from begging"), old age, the strongest ("Those who are satisfied have rented themselves out for bread"), need ("Friend, give me three breads") and the saint friend ("you should rather ask those who sell them.").

7 – *Saint Antoine of Padua*. The window presents four superimposed scenes of the life of the Franciscan born in 1195 and who died in 1231. At the bottom you can see him first among the crowd, he is holding the Saint Sacrament and a mule is kneeling. At the forefront two donors are kneeling, and at the back at the left of the three towers there is a nave . A second scene represents the saint preaching at the funeral of an usurer on "where your treasure is, your heart will be" (Luke, XII, 34). A dog is playing near the coffin and the privy purse of the deceased is opened : his heart is inside. A young

man who had hit his mother is represented, saint Antoine having pronounced this verse of the Scripture : "If your foot scandalizes you, cut it" , he mutilates himself but was soon cured by the saint. Finally, the top of the window is devoted to the death of the saint.

8 – Under the previous window the window of the saints was placed, with a very architectural composition presenting six large characters on three levels. Its is read from top to bottom and from left to right. In the tympan are God the Father and the dove of the Holy Spirit. First there is saint Vincent as a deacon with three swords, the patron of the parish, then saint James the major dressed as a pilgrim. In the intermediate level, again under a nice Renaissance arch, an archbishop who has not been identified and saint Nicholas recognizable from the salting tub from which he has pulled three children that the buitcher was going to kill and cut into pieces. At the bottom, are saint John the Baptist and saint Anne who is teaching the Virgin how to read. Under them the donors are kneeling.

9 – *The childhood and the public life of Christ* combine stories of the Gospel with those of the Apocryphal book. The glass which was placed in the ambulatory of the choir of Saint-Vincent opens the cycle devoted to Christ. The tympan is itself a rich composition, since it presents, among the angels, the Annunciation ("Hail Mary full of grace, the Lord is with you") and the dove of the Holy Spirit perched on a bouquet of lilies (symbol of purity). The stained-glass window is then organized on two levels in four lancets. At the top left is celebrated, under the Trinity, the Immaculate Conception, with on a strip : "You are beautiful..." (Song of Songs, IV, 7). Then comes Nativity under a very ornate column, while the shepherds are in the fields and are written the words sung by the angels on the night of Christmas : "*Gloria in excelsis Deo and pax hominibus bonae voluntatis.*" Arrive the Wise men directed by the star. Gaspard kneels to kiss Jesus' foot while the two others speak with Joseph and show him the star.. Then there is the presentation at the Temple whose architecture reminds the churches of that period, as the one of Caudebec which also

*The nativity*

has a hanging keystone. At the foot of the altar are the lamb and the turtledoves for the sacrifice. At the bottom left, the Saint Family exposed to the revenge of Herod, flees to Egypt and the wheat is just sown that it comes up by miracle. Jesus is then represented at the age of 12, among the doctors of the Temple of Jerusalem. With his mother, he is at the wedding feast at Cana where he changes water into wine, the first of his miracles. Then his public life starts after the thirty first years of his hidden life in Nazareth. He then bids farewell to his mother.

10 – *The Passion* can be read from bottom to top and from left to right. The first scene is the entry of Christ on a mule in Jerusalem in the middle of the crowd which contrasts with the solitude in the Garden of Gethsamane which follows it. Christ is kneeling and praying, an angel comforts him while in the foreground the apostles have dozed off. Then an army comes to arrest him, Jude kisses him and Peter threatens Malchus, the servant of the great priest, with his sword and is about to cut his ear. Christ then appears before Caiphe, the great priest. The upper register opens by the flagellation of Christ who is then presented by Pontius Pilate to the crowd of Jews ("*Ecce*

*The Passion of the Christ*

*homo*", here is man). The latter are asking for death, Pilate who represents the Roman authority and has found nothing guilty in Christ, washes his hands. Handed over to his accusers, Christ, sentenced to be crucified, goes up towards Calvary, carrying his cross with the help of Joseph of Arimathy. In the tympan, God the Father sits enthroned in his glory dominating the coat of arms of the donors and in other openwork, Veronica presenting the veil with the face of Christ as well as angels carrying the instruments of Passion.

*Passion and Crucifixion*

There is also Malchus' lantern, the sponge which was used to drink vinegar, Longin's spear, the Roman centurion who stabbed Christ's side and saw water come out, the thorned crown, the whip and the birch, Jude's privy purse, Peter's sword and Malchus' ear, and at last the reed which was the sceptre given to Christ by derision to stress his title of "king of the Jews".

11 – *The Crucifixion* spreads out over the window , two levels and three lancets. In the tympan, Christ of the Last Judgment sits and towards him are turned kneeling the Virgin and saint John who were present at the Crucifixion. Behind them is the crowd of people who rose from the Dead. Under the sun and the moon, the crucified Christ is surrounded by the good and the bad thief, also crucified. But above the cross of Christ a pelican is perched. The bird who has sacrified itself for its young, giving itself as food, is an allegory of Christ and the Eucharist. In the background, architectures suggest how close Jerusalem is. On the left are the Virgin and saint John with the saint women, while Madeleine, recognizable with her perfume vase, is kneeling at the foot of the cross. On the right, soldiers are supervising the location. At the foot of the window, donors are kneeling on both sides of a cartouche which bears the inscription : "*O Mater Dei memento mei* (O ! Mother of God, remember me)."

12 – *Resurrection and apparitions* are the theme of the next window. It starts at the top left by the Deposition. Prostrate with grief, the Virgin is supported by saint John. Christ is then entombed. He rises from the dead on the third day, arising from the tomb despite the soldiers standing guard. Then the saint women arrive, among them Madeleine with her tousled hair. In the lower register, Christ, surrounded by angels, appears to his mother in a scene which had already been represented before in the Saint-Godard church in Rouen. Again carrying a cross with the standard of the resurrection, he shows himself to Madeleine. Then he accompanies the two pilgrims of Emmaus who left Jerusalem and, in the inn (with its rich Renaissance decoration), after explaining to them the passages of the Scripture announcing his death and his resurrec-

*Resurrection and the apparitions of Christ*

tion, he breaks the bread. They recognize him then and he disappears . Finally, he appears before saint Thomas the non believer and has him touch the holes of the nails in his hands and the wound of his side. In the tympan the glory of the Trinity bursts : God the Father carries the tiara and holds the globe, the Son, the cross – both sign of ignonimy and of his victory over death -, the Holy Spirit here being represented with a human face.

13 – *The martyrdom of saint Vincent* is exceptionally rich. To honour with the most dignity possible the saint patron of the parish, the iconography based itself both on the *Acta Sanctorum* and the *Golden Legend*. At the bottom left, Vincent the deacon who took the defence of the bishop Valere, is led before the proconsul Dacien. Sentenced, both men are taken to gaol. Vincent is roasted alive and one of his executioners sticks a fork in his entrails. Then he is fixed on a cross of Saint-Andrew, and then is carded with iron cards which tear him. But his suffering goes on since after he is crushed under the

*The martyrdom of saint Vincent*

screw of a press, there is a scene introduced by the persons who ordered the window, while it is not mentioned in any other written source. The martyr is seen dying on a bed. His executioners want to get rid of his body, they throw him in the middle of the sea with a millstone around his neck, in vain, because his body keeps on floating. Washed up on the shore, he is protected by a crow who keeps wild animals away which have come to dismember him.

The tympan is devoted to the Lithanies of the Virgin. The prayer which gives several allegorical names to Mary whose protection and intercession are besought, is illustrated, in strips, by the starfish, the moon, the lily among the thorns, the fountain and the enclosed garden.

*Details of the vitrail des chars*

# BIBLIOGRAPHY


A. ROBINNE, *Le Vieux-Marché de Rouen, 1431-1966*, Rouen, 1966.

*Le Vieux-Marché de Rouen*, numéro spécial du *Bulletin des Amis des Monuments Rouennais*, juillet 1978-mai 1979, avec notamment les contributions de J.-P. Bardet, J.-P. Chaline et de F. Perrot.

F. PERROT, « Le vitrail à Rouen », *Connaître Rouen*, t.II, Rouen, 1972.

N. PROUIN, *Courbes et contre-courbes*, Rouen, 1984.

C. BRISAC, *Le vitrail*, Paris, 1990.

*Rouen. Église Sainte-Jeanne-d'Arc, les verrières*, Itinéraires du patrimoine, 67, Rouen, 1994.

*Vitraux retrouvés de Saint-Vincent de Rouen*, Catalogue d'exposition, Rouen, 1995.

*Statue of saint Joan of Arc, Michel Cose, sculptor, 1999.*

To celebrate the twentieth years of the church, on the 25th April 1999, Monseigneur Duval, archbishop of Rouen, blessed a bronze statue of saint Joan of Arc, made by the sculptor Michel Coste.

The sculpture of saint Joan of Arc expresses her radiant presence **from her sky, transfigured** – an expression full of softness and amiability.

Here Joan is the welcome and the invitation to join her in her **happiness as a woman** – a woman with a **face full of innocence** and henceforth accomplished, "she entered the joy of her Lord (1)", in their **nuptials of fire**.

Thus, Joan is a **good news angel** reporting to us set against the backdrop of misfortune and war, the surprising **"message of peace"** of the Gospel (2) : she, whose courage and struggles were driven by the ardent desire of giving her own the happiness promised.

Then Joan testifies to another meaning of her ordeal, where there are only flames of the stake and the **fire of love** she seems flared up with (3) and in which she takes us and welcomes us.

---

(1) Mt 25, 21
(2) Lc 19, 42 ; Os. 2, 20.
(3) Mt 3, 11 ; Ex. 3, 2 ; Cant 8, 6.

# PHOTO CREDITS

Guy Bouvard, p. 8, 10, 12, 17, 20, 21, 22, 24, 25, 32 et couverture
Pierre Fauvel, p. 23 haut
Brigitte Dubois, p. 23 bas
Philippe Poirson, p. 38
Inventaire du Patrimoine :
Thierry Leroy, Spadem, p. 29, 35, 39, 42, et p. 34, 44
Denis Couchaux, 1988, Spadem, p. 40
Michel Coste, p. 46

Achevé d'imprimer par Corlet, Imprimeur, S.A.
14110 Condé-sur-Noireau
N° d'Imprimeur : 86853 - Dépôt légal : septembre 2005

*Imprimé en France.*